The Diary of a Young Girl

Lightbox Literature Studies

Michelle Lomberg and Katie Gillespie

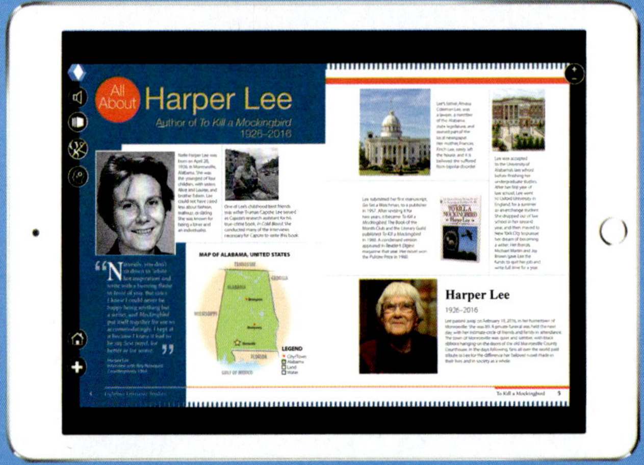

Lightbox is an all-inclusive digital solution for the teaching and learning of curriculum topics in an original, groundbreaking way. Lightbox is based on National Curriculum Standards.

STANDARD FEATURES OF LIGHTBOX

AUDIO High-quality narration using text-to-speech system

VIDEOS Embedded high-definition video clips

ACTIVITIES Printable PDFs that can be emailed and graded

WEBLINKS Curated links to external, child-safe resources

SLIDESHOWS Pictorial overviews of key concepts

TRANSPARENCIES Step-by-step layering of maps, diagrams, charts, and timelines

INTERACTIVE MAPS Interactive maps and aerial satellite imagery

QUIZZES Ten multiple choice questions that are automatically graded and emailed for teacher assessment

KEY WORDS Matching key concepts to their definitions

MORE Extra information and details on the subject

FIRST HAND Letters, diaries, and other primary sources

DOCS Speeches, newspaper articles, and other historical documents

Contents

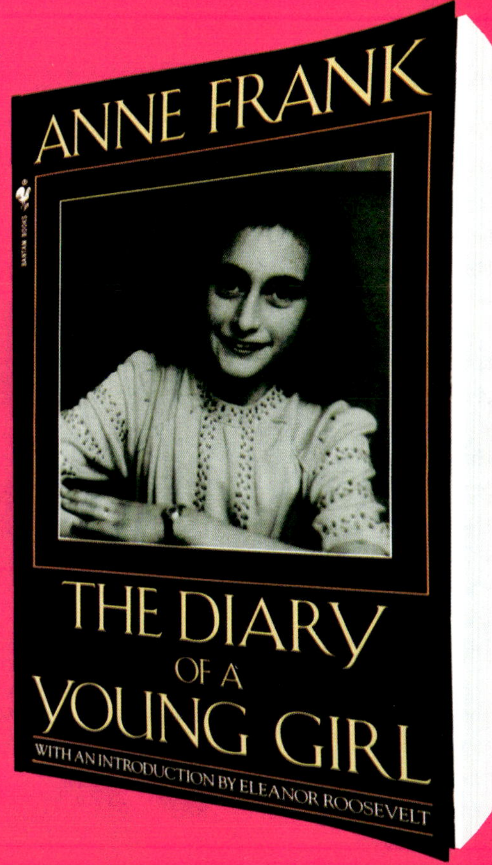

2 Access Lightbox Student Edition
4 All About Anne Frank
6 Setting of the Diary
8 Time Period of the Diary
10 Conflict in the Diary
12 Introducing the Characters
14 The Art of Storytelling
16 Theme in the Diary
18 Symbolism in the Diary
20 The Use of Language
22 Impact of the Diary at the Time of Publishing
24 Impact of the Diary Now
26 Perspectives on Genocide
28 Writing a Comparative Essay
30 Key Words/Literary Terms
31 Index
32 Log on to www.openlightbox.com

RUBRIC

Conducting an Interview

Students will conduct an interview with a community member about a time period in their community's history, and submit an audio recording and transcript of the interview. An exemplary interview will meet the following criteria.

- Clearly defines the purpose of the interview
- Conducts thorough background research to inform the focus of the interview and the questions
- Drafts a complete list of thoughtful, in-depth, and varied questions prior to the interview
- Interviews a subject with relevant knowledge on the topic and time period in question
- Asks questions in a logical order, building upon each other
- Treats the interview subject in a polite, respectful, and professional manner
- Does not interrupt or rush the interview subject
- Shows interest and enthusiasm in responses and follow-up questions
- Chooses follow-up questions that demonstrate active listening
- Asks for clarification and further details when necessary
- Asks questions about personal experiences related to the topic
- Asks questions regarding factual information and the interview subject's opinion on the topic
- Asks creative questions that reflect fresh insights on the topic
- Records the full interview in a quiet environment
- Organizes and edits the interview transcript to be clear and factual

Anne Frank

1929–1945

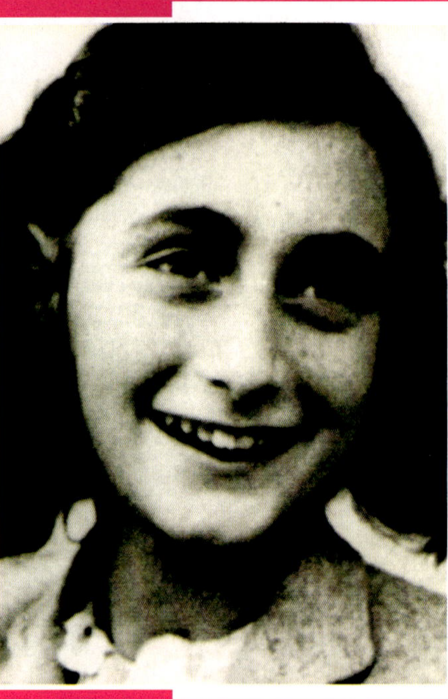

Annelies Marie Frank was born in Frankfurt am Main, Germany, on June 12, 1929. She had a sister, Margot, who was three years older. Her father, Otto Frank, was a banker and businessman who could trace his family's history in Frankfurt to the seventeenth century. Her mother, Edith, came from a well-off family in Aachen, Germany. Edith and Otto were married in 1925. Although the Franks followed Jewish traditions, they were not strict observers of the faith.

Anne's early years in Germany were happy. Edith watched over the girls as they played with neighborhood friends. Otto, nicknamed Pim, made up stories to entertain his daughters at bedtime. Their lives changed in 1933, however, when Adolf Hitler came to power. The new government enacted anti-Jewish measures immediately. Otto and Edith decided to move the family to the Netherlands, where they settled in Amsterdam. Anne and Margot thrived in their new schools.

> **"It's an odd idea for someone like me to keep a diary; not only because I have never done so before, but because it seems to me that neither I—nor for that matter anyone else—will be interested in the unbosomings of a thirteen-year-old schoolgirl. Still, what does that matter? I want to write, but more than that, I want to bring out all kinds of things that lie buried deep in my heart."**
>
> Saturday, 20 June, 1942
> *The Diary of a Young Girl*

MAP OF GERMANY AND THE NETHERLANDS

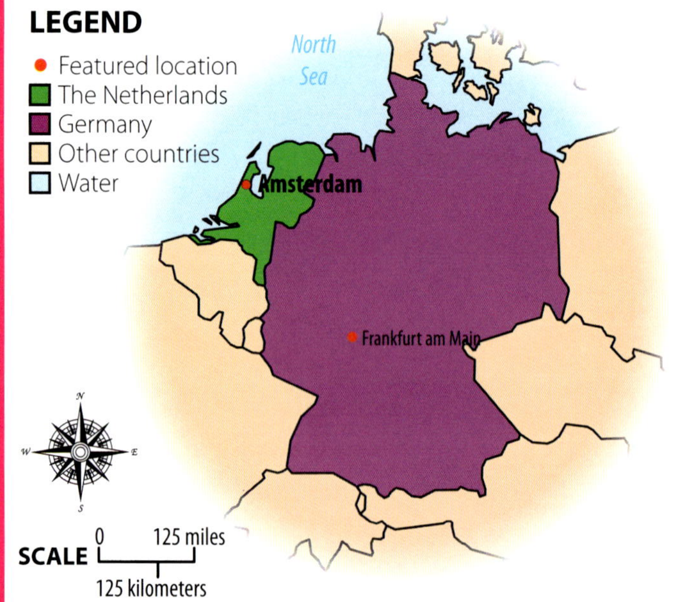

The Franks' peaceful time in Amsterdam came to an end in May 1940 when German forces attacked and occupied the Netherlands. Otto and Edith understood that the **anti-Semitic** policies of the new **regime** could put the family in danger, so Otto attempted to get the family out of the Netherlands. Since he was unable to obtain visas in time, Otto arranged a hiding place instead—the Secret Annex—behind his workplace. A few weeks after Anne's thirteenth birthday, the family relocated there.

Anne had received a diary for her thirteenth birthday. More than just a written record, the diary, which she called "Kitty," became Anne's best friend and confidante. Anne poured out her grievances, hopes, and dreams on its pages. An avid writer, Anne also penned stories and kept a book of favorite quotes.

The Van Pels family, referred to as the Van Daan family in Anne's diary, and later another acquaintance, joined the Franks in the Secret Annex. The group had to remain quiet during the day when workers were in the building. After working hours, the families followed a schedule of meals, lessons, chores, and sleep.

The eight occupants of the Secret Annex lived there for two years, never setting foot outside. On August 4, 1944, they were arrested, along with two outside helpers. The eight who had been in hiding were sent to Westerbork, a transit camp in the Netherlands. In September, they were transferred to Auschwitz, the infamous **concentration camp** in Poland. There, the men were separated from the women. Anne never saw her beloved Pim again. Weeks later, Margot and Anne were sent to Bergen-Belsen, a concentration camp in Germany. Edith, who was unwell, was left behind at Auschwitz, where she died on January 6, 1945. Anne and Margot died of typhus, likely in February 1945. Otto was the only member of the Frank family to survive. He returned to Amsterdam, where he published Anne's diary in 1947.

ACTIVITIES

Google Maps

Anne Frank House, Amsterdam, Netherlands
Explore the site of the museum dedicated to Anne Frank, using street view.

Weblink

Introducing 'Anne Frank House VR,' an Immersive Experience that Recreates Amsterdam's Secret Annex and Preserves a Piece of Holocaust History
Examine the blog post by Oculus VR posted on June 12, 2018.

1. How do the goals of this project align with Anne's vision? Do you think she would approve of this experience? Support your answer by citing evidence from the diary.
2. Why do you think there is a demand for this type of experience? How might it help audiences of today to better connect with Anne's story?

RUBRIC

Researching for a Writing Assignment

Students will complete a thorough research process to prepare for a writing assignment, and organize their research in a logical manner that supports their writing. An exemplary research process will meet the following criteria.

- Creates a goal for the research, based on the topic and working thesis
- Creates specific, thoughtful, and inventive research questions that are relevant to the topic of the writing assignment
- Produces a list of categories, key words, and related ideas to effectively assist in researching
- Uses high-quality sources that pertain to the topic and come in a variety of formats, such as books, journals, primary sources, websites, and databases
- Determines accuracy of all sources
- Uses sources that provide balanced research and various perspectives on the topic in question
- Takes notes to highlight the key facts and ideas in order to answer all research questions
- Extracts relevant, detailed information from the sources during the note-taking process
- Organizes the research notes in a clear and concise manner
- Organizes the research notes logically and in a way that sets up the information and ideas for analysis and the writing process
- Analyzes the information and produces ideas and points to support the working thesis
- Uses an effective and suitable format to present all research
- Properly cites all sources used

Setting of the Diary

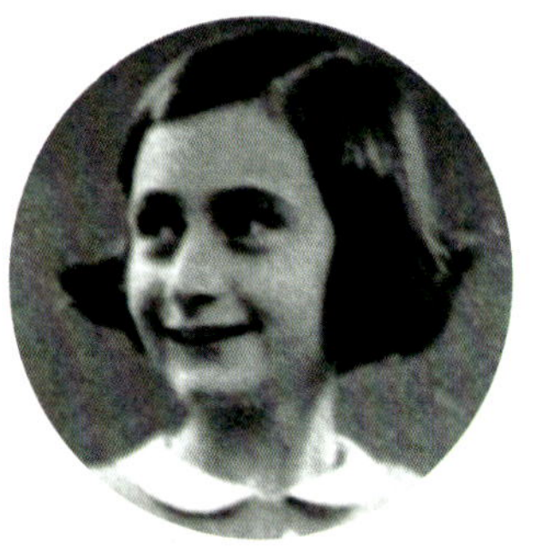

The Diary of a Young Girl is set in Amsterdam, the capital city of the Netherlands. The Netherlands lies between the North Sea and Germany's northwestern border, with Belgium on its southern border. German forces invaded the small country on May 10, 1940. After less than a week of fighting, following the devastating bombing of Rotterdam, the country surrendered. Nevertheless, the Dutch people put up a fierce resistance to their oppressors, organizing general strikes, helping Jews hide or escape, and providing **intelligence** to the Allied Forces. The group in hiding feared the bombing raids and eagerly listened to the radio for news of the Allied Forces' advancements.

Amsterdam is located in the province of North Holland. The city lies slightly below sea level and has many miles (km) of canals. In 1941, Amsterdam was home to approximately 79,000 Jews—less than 10 percent of the population. Of these, more than 10,000 were **refugees**, who, like the Frank family, had fled there in the 1930s.

Snapshot

The Netherlands in World War II

159,806 Jews registered themselves in **1941**, as required by the German occupying authorities.

On **February 25, 1941**, Dutch workers began a **general strike** to protest the Nazi treatment of Jews.

Between **25,000** and **30,000** Dutch Jews went into hiding. Of those, **two-thirds survived**.

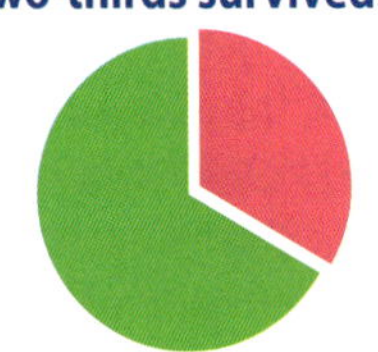

Less than 25 percent of Jews in the Netherlands **survived World War II**.

The Hiding Place

"If I just think of how we live here, I usually come to the conclusion that it is a paradise compared with how other Jews who are not in hiding must be living."

Saturday, 1 May, 1943, *The Diary of a Young Girl*

From December 1933, until they went into hiding in July 1942, the family lived in apartment number 37 on the Merwedeplein square. Anne and Margot made many friends on the square, some of whom were also Jewish refugees from Germany. Anne attended a **Montessori school**, where Otto felt she got the individual attention she needed. The first 10 diary entries are set in the Frank family home. Anne wrote the rest of her diary while hiding in the Secret Annex. The hiding place was an empty part of the building where Otto worked, located at Prinsengracht 263, on one of Amsterdam's main canals. The business operated as usual in the front of the building, while the suite of rooms in the back concealed the people in hiding.

The Secret Annex had four floors. A kitchen and office took up the bottom floor. During workdays, workers used the kitchen for product testing. After hours, the residents went there to fetch hot water for their baths. They gathered in the office to listen to news and music on the radio. On the second floor, a moving bookcase connected the Secret Annex with the rest of the building. The bedroom that Anne shared with Dussel was on this floor, as was the Franks' sitting room, which doubled as a bedroom for Edith, Otto, and Margot. A tiny bathroom, with only a toilet and sink, was used by all eight residents. The Van Daans occupied the third floor. Peter's room was a tiny landing under the stairs to the attic. Mr. and Mrs. Van Daan's room was the largest in the annex. Formerly used as a laboratory, it had a sink and stove, and served not only as the Van Daans' bedroom, but also as a kitchen, dining room, and sitting room for the whole group. The attic was used for storing food. It had a window with a view of a chestnut tree. Anne went to the attic to look out the window, spend time with Peter, and write.

ACTIVITIES

Video

Who Was Anne Frank? | History

Learn more about Anne Frank by watching this video.

1. It is said in the video that Anne "wrote with a wit and an awareness well beyond her years." How does Anne's maturity come through in her writing? Cite specific examples from the diary.
2. The setting of Anne's story comes from her own real-life experiences. How do you think the diary would be different if it were written somewhere else? What do you think Anne would have written about if she had been able to take her diary with her when the family was discovered? How might the tone of the diary have changed?

First Hand

Richard Dimbleby Describes Belsen

Listen to Richard Dimbleby's account of the concentration camp where Anne and Margo Frank died in 1945.

1. Initially, the BBC refused to broadcast Dimbleby's report until he threatened to resign if they did not. Why would he resort to such extreme measures to ensure his report was aired? How do you think this report was received by the public when it was first broadcast in 1945?
2. How does hearing this description of the camp affect your understanding of what Anne and her family, along with millions of others, were forced to endure? Why is it so important to tell stories like this, even if they are difficult to hear?

Time Period of the Diary

The Diary of a Young Girl spans the period from Sunday, June 14, 1942 to Tuesday, August 1, 1944. World War II was raging across Europe during this time. When Anne and her family went into hiding, German troops had occupied the Netherlands for two years and had imposed increasingly severe restrictions on Jews. The Secret Annex group spent its time in hiding, waiting for the Allied invasion that would drive the Nazis from the Netherlands and end the war.

Anti-Semitism in the Netherlands

"After May 1940 good times rapidly fled: first the war, then the capitulation, followed by the arrival of the Germans, which is when the suffering of us Jews really began. Anti-Jewish decrees followed each other in quick succession. Jews must wear a yellow star, Jews must hand in their bicycles, Jews are banned from trams and are forbidden to drive. Jews are only allowed to do their shopping between three and five o'clock and then only in shops which bear the placard 'Jewish shop.' Jews must be indoors by eight o'clock and cannot even sit in their own gardens after that hour. Jews are forbidden to visit theaters, cinemas, and other places of entertainment. Jews may not take part in public sports. Swimming baths, tennis courts, hockey fields, and other sports grounds are all prohibited to them. Jews may not visit Christians. Jews must go to Jewish schools, and many more restrictions of a similar kind."

Saturday, 20 June, 1942, *The Diary of a Young Girl*

World War II had many causes, but German resentment of the Treaty of Versailles, which ended World War I, coupled with economic troubles following the Great Depression, set the stage for the rise of Hitler and the Nazi party. The war began when Germany invaded Poland on September 1, 1939, prompting Great Britain and France to declare war on Germany. The Allied nations, including Great Britain and the British Commonwealth, France, the Soviet Union, and the United States, battled the Axis forces—mainly Germany, Italy, and Japan. During six years of warfare, it is estimated that 35 to 70 million military personnel and **civilians** lost their lives. The war, which had spread to Africa and Asia, ended on September 2, 1945, when Japan surrendered.

Persecution of **minorities** was a defining policy of Nazi rule. Hitler believed that German and other northern European people belonged to the Aryan race. The Aryans, according to Nazi belief, were a superior race, and needed more territory and resources in order to flourish. As the Nazis invaded and occupied country after country, they sought to eliminate not only Jews, but also Roma, Slavs, black people, homosexuals, people with disabilities, and political **dissidents**. Jews and others were driven from their homes and imprisoned in concentration camps, where they were murdered in gas chambers, starved, or worked to death. 6 million Jewish people lost their lives during the **Holocaust**.

ACTIVITIES

Video

Anne Frank's step-sister opens up about their extraordinary story

Find out more about Anne and the Holocaust by watching this interview with her friend, and later step-sister, Eva Schloss.

1. In the video, Schloss talks about how Anne liked writing and was known for telling stories. What evidence of this can you see in her diary? How successful is Anne as a storyteller? Give examples from the text.
2. How did the time period that *The Diary of a Young Girl* was written in impact Anne's creation of the diary? In what ways might the story be different if it were written today?

Weblink

Anne's Timeline

Examine the timeline to learn more about the historical events connected with Anne's story.

1. Anne received the diary as a birthday gift, and began writing in it only a few weeks before her family was forced into hiding. How, if at all, does Anne's writing change from her first entry to her last entry? What effect does the inclusion of her diary entries before entering the Secret Annex have on the reader's perception of the diary as a whole?
2. The concentration camp at Bergen-Belsen where Anne and her sister Margo were held was liberated by British troops only a few weeks after their deaths from typhus. Do you think Anne's diary would still have been published, had she survived the war? Why or why not?

RUBRIC

Writing a Short Story

Students will choose an excerpt from the diary and use it as their inspiration in writing a short story. An exemplary short story will meet the following criteria.

- Engages the reader from the opening line
- Establishes a clear, consistent point of view
- Introduces a narrator and a setting
- Develops an engaging conflict at the heart of the narrative to build tension and keep the reader interested
- Develops characters and events through purposeful and well-crafted literary devices
- Creates a logical progression of events in the narrative that build upon each other using various techniques
- Explores ideas, concepts, and writing styles with creativity and originality
- Demonstrates a high level of skill in using appropriate narrative techniques to tell the story
- Concludes the narrative in a thoughtful, effective manner appropriate to the narrative
- Uses varied, purposeful diction and syntax to affect style and serve the narrative
- Writes with clarity, imagination, and a unique, personal voice
- Does not use stereotypes or clichés
- Uses effective, believable dialogue
- Uses correct spelling, grammar, and punctuation

Conflict in the Diary

Conflict is the foundation of any story, even a non-fiction story such as a memoir. Conflicts arise in a narrative when the main character, or protagonist, is threatened or prevented from reaching his or her goals. These obstacles may be external, or they may come from within the main character. More than one conflict can be present in a story.

The Four Major Types of Conflict in Literature

MAN VS. MAN

In a man versus man conflict, the protagonist faces opposition from another character, called the antagonist. The antagonist may thwart the protagonist's attempts to reach a goal, or even threaten the protagonist's life. In the *Harry Potter* series, Harry repeatedly battles Lord Voldemort for his own survival and for the good of the wizarding world.

MAN VS. SELF

In a man versus self conflict, the main character struggles with his or her own feelings or beliefs. In *Macbeth*, both Macbeth and Lady Macbeth struggle with their own consciences. Even though they have achieved their goal of ruling Scotland, they cannot enjoy the power that this position brings because they are tormented by guilt over how they got there.

MAN VS. SOCIETY

In a man versus society conflict, the main character is in conflict with the norms or prejudices in his or her society. One of the conflicts in *A Raisin in the Sun* is between the Younger family and the white community, represented by Mr. Lindner. He expresses the **racism** prevalent in society when he makes it clear that the Youngers are not welcome in their new neighborhood.

MAN VS. NATURE

In a man versus nature conflict, the main character is in a battle against the forces of nature, which may take the form of a hostile landscape, climate, animal, or natural disaster. *Into Thin Air* chronicles the struggles of a group of mountain climbers. They face blinding storms and altitude sickness on their ill-fated ascent of Mount Everest.

ACTIVITIES

Types of Conflict in *The Diary of a Young Girl*

When eight people spend two years hiding in cramped quarters to evade capture and death, conflict is inevitable. In her diary, Anne Frank depicts three main types of conflict. These include man versus society, man versus man, and man versus self. Each conflict occurs repeatedly as Anne describes the tensions that arise in the Secret Annex.

Man versus Society

"To our great horror and regret we hear that the attitude of a great many people towards us Jews has changed. We hear that there is anti-Semitism now in circles that never thought of it before. This news has affected us all very, very deeply. The cause of this hatred of the Jews is understandable, even human sometimes, but not good. The Christians blame the Jews for giving secrets away to the Germans, for betraying their helpers and for the fact that...a great many Christians have gone the way of so many others before them, and suffered terrible punishments and a dreadful fate."

Monday, 22 May, 1944, *The Diary of a Young Girl*

Man versus Man

"I was seething with rage, and thought Dussel frightfully rude (which he certainly was) and myself very friendly. In the evening when I could get hold of Pim, I told him how it had gone off and discussed what I should do next, because I was not going to give in, and preferred to clear it up myself. Pim told me how I ought to tackle the problem, but warned me that it would be better to leave it till the next day, as I was so het up."

Tuesday, 13 July, 1943, *The Diary of a Young Girl*

Man versus Self

"I am afraid of myself, I am afraid that in my longing I am giving myself too quickly. How, later on, can it ever go right with other boys? Oh, it is so difficult, always battling with one's heart and reason; in its own time, each will speak, but do I know for certain that I have chosen the right time?"

Friday, 28 April, 1944, *The Diary of a Young Girl*

More

The Types of Conflict in *The Diary of a Young Girl*

Analyze the excerpts from the diary revealing the types of conflict as they appear in *The Diary of a Young Girl*.

1. How do these excerpts of conflict reveal the diary's theme? How do they reveal character? Explain and defend your ideas.
2. Write an analysis of Anne's development of conflict between herself and Dussel. What deeper truths may be suggested about these characters as a result of their conflict?

Weblink

New pages from Anne Frank's Diary reveal family conflict

Learn more about the Frank family by reading this article from *The Guardian*.

1. Otto Frank always acknowledged that the original published diary was incomplete, due to concerns over offending people still living. How does Anne's conflict with her mother affect the way you perceive both characters? Why?
2. Why do you think Otto wanted these five pages made public after he and his second wife died? What, if anything, does knowledge of this conflict in Otto and Edith's marriage change about your opinion of the Frank family?

RUBRIC

Holding a Classroom Debate

Students will form groups and prepare arguments for a debate on a controversial issue. Exemplary performance in a debate will meet the following criteria.

- Demonstrates in-depth understanding of the topic and related information
- Presents strong, logical, and convincing arguments
- Communicates in a clear and confident manner
- Maintains eye contact
- Uses clear vocal tone and a reasonable rate of vocal delivery
- Uses respectful and appropriate language and body language
- Delivers arguments, evidence, and counter-evidence in an engaging and persuasive manner
- Supports each major point of an argument with several relevant and detailed facts and examples
- Connects all arguments to the overall topic in a clear, concise, and organized manner
- Presents the arguments and supporting evidence in a clear, logical manner
- Presents clear, thorough, and accurate information throughout the debate
- Addresses all of the opposing team's arguments with counter-arguments
- Identifies any weakness in the opposing team's arguments
- Constructs strong and relevant counter-arguments using accurate information
- Presents strong and persuasive arguments throughout the debate
- Summarizes the arguments in the closing statement

Introducing the Characters

Readers learn about characters in literature by what they say, what they do, and what others say about them. Authors can present characters indirectly, by showing the reader their words and actions, leaving the reader to draw conclusions. Authors can also describe characters directly from their own perspectives or from the narrator's point of view.

Major Characters in *The Diary of a Young Girl*

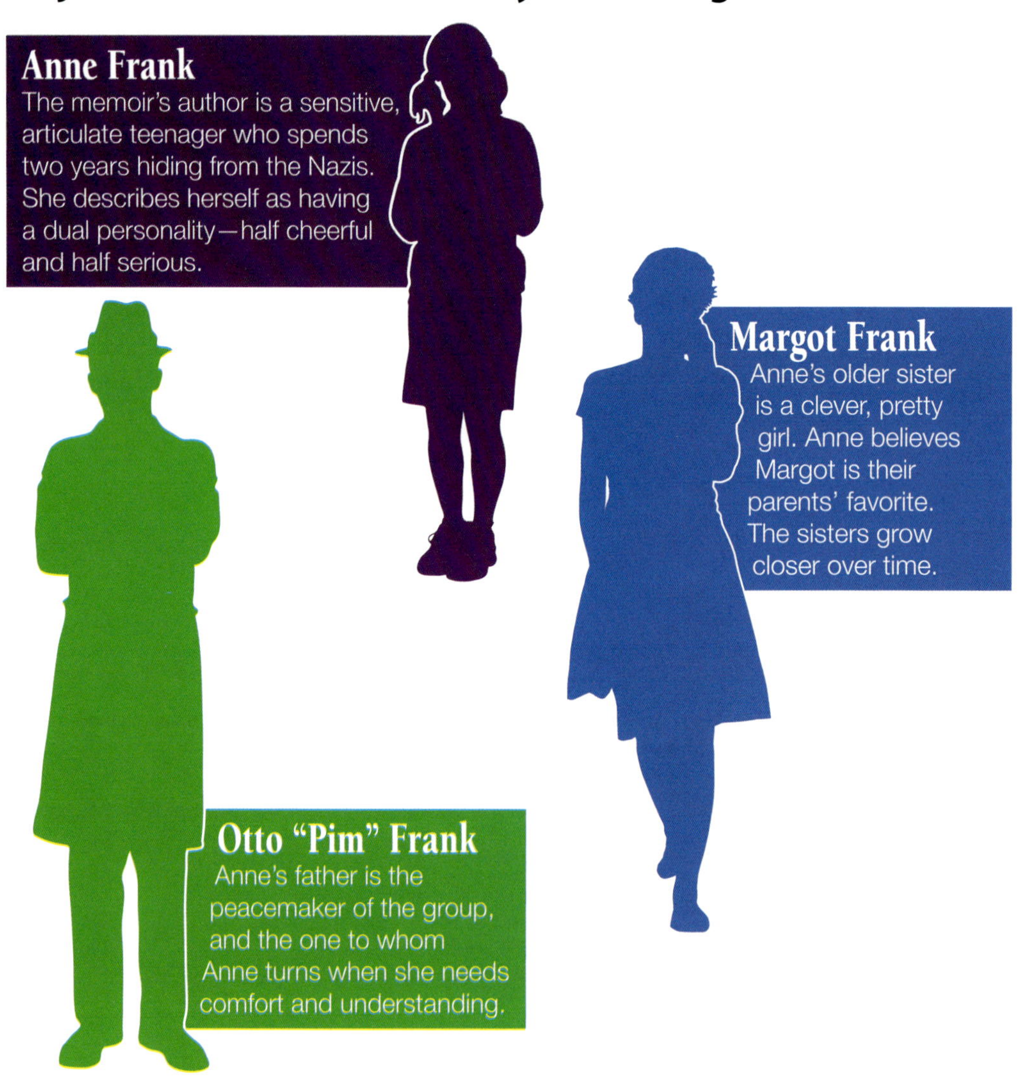

Anne Frank
The memoir's author is a sensitive, articulate teenager who spends two years hiding from the Nazis. She describes herself as having a dual personality—half cheerful and half serious.

Margot Frank
Anne's older sister is a clever, pretty girl. Anne believes Margot is their parents' favorite. The sisters grow closer over time.

Otto "Pim" Frank
Anne's father is the peacemaker of the group, and the one to whom Anne turns when she needs comfort and understanding.

Anne introduces the people around her to the reader, indirectly by reporting their speech and actions, and directly by giving her candid opinions about them. The reader sees the characters only through Anne's eyes, and does not have access to other characters' unspoken thoughts and emotions. Unlike diarists, writers of fiction can use the third-person point of view to show readers what their characters are thinking.

Most stories are organized around a conflict between a protagonist and one or more antagonists. In *The Diary of a Young Girl*, Anne is both the narrator and the protagonist. Her main goal, and that of the others in hiding, is to survive the Holocaust. She has conflicts with her mother and with others in the Secret Annex. She also wrestles with internal conflicts, as she experiences love for the first time, and wonders about her place in the world.

Some characters, called static characters, remain unchanged over the course of a story. Other characters, called dynamic characters, change as a result of the events in the story. The main character is almost always a dynamic character.

ACTIVITIES

Weblink

Character Analysis of Peter Van Daan

Review a character analysis of Peter and debate his role in *The Diary of Anne Frank*.

1. At first, Anne does not think much of Peter, but she comes to care more for him later on. Why does Anne's opinion of Peter change over the course of the diary? How does this affect the reader's opinion of him?
2. How do you think Anne and Peter's relationship would have been different if they were not confined to the Secret Annex? Explain why you think so by giving textual evidence from the diary.

More

Character Development in *The Diary of a Young Girl*

Analyze the characters in *The Diary of a Young Girl* using the descriptions on the character map and excerpts from each character. Then, choose a character and answer the following questions.

1. Which of the writer's techniques are most effective at revealing this character's traits? Why?
2. In what ways is the characterization of this character ineffective? What could be done to improve this character's function in the diary? Defend your ideas with evidence.

RUBRIC

Creating a Literary Device Analysis Booklet

Students will analyze the author's use of a literary device in the diary, and create a booklet to present this analysis. An exemplary literary device analysis booklet will meet the following criteria.

- Defines the chosen literary device accurately and in detail
- Places the definition of the literary device at the beginning of the booklet
- Provides strong, specific examples of how this literary device is used in the diary
- Describes examples in detail, with quotations properly integrated
- Includes thorough analysis of the use, purpose, and effectiveness of each example of how the chosen literary device is used in the diary
- Arranges all pages logically
- Examples are organized chronologically
- Provides no more than one example and its analysis per page
- Creates a neat, well-organized, and attractive booklet
- Booklet is colorful and displays the student's creativity
- Uses illustrations to represent the chosen literary device and the examples of how it is used in the diary

The Art of Storytelling

Storytelling is an art that has entertained, informed, inspired, and persuaded listeners and readers since ancient times. Writers can use many different literary devices to craft their narratives. Anne Frank uses a number of literary devices in her diary to develop character and convey mood.

Structure of a Narrative

Freytag's Pyramid is a model of how plots are commonly structured. *The Diary of a Young Girl* as a whole does not follow the structure of Freytag's Pyramid. However, some entries within the diary, such as the burglary Anne recounts in her Tuesday, April 11, 1944, entry, have all the elements of the pyramid.

Freytag's Pyramid

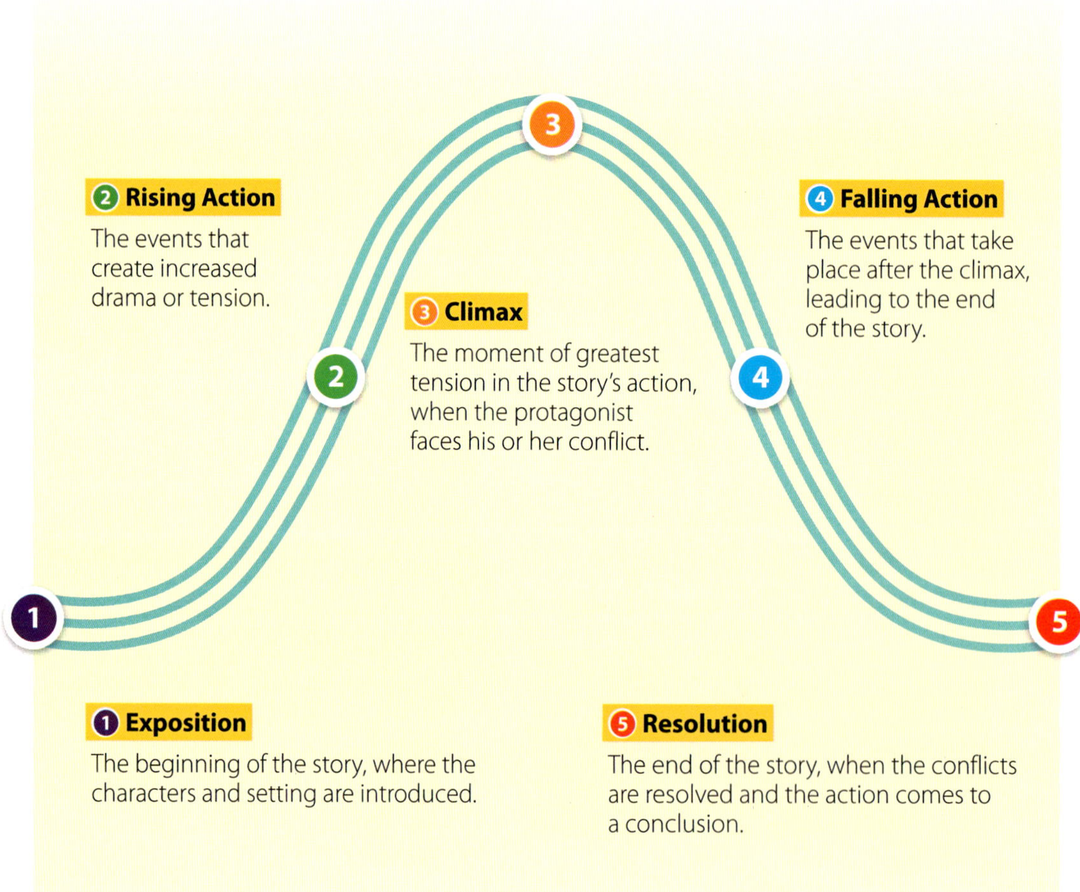

Plot

Whatever form it takes, a story needs a plot—a sequence of events with a beginning, a middle, and an end. An author may tell a story out of order, beginning in the middle and using flashback and flash-forward techniques. Nevertheless, events in the plotline—the order in which events take place in time—must follow each other in a logical sequence.

Plot Points from 5 July, 1942 to 14 August, 1942, of Anne's Diary

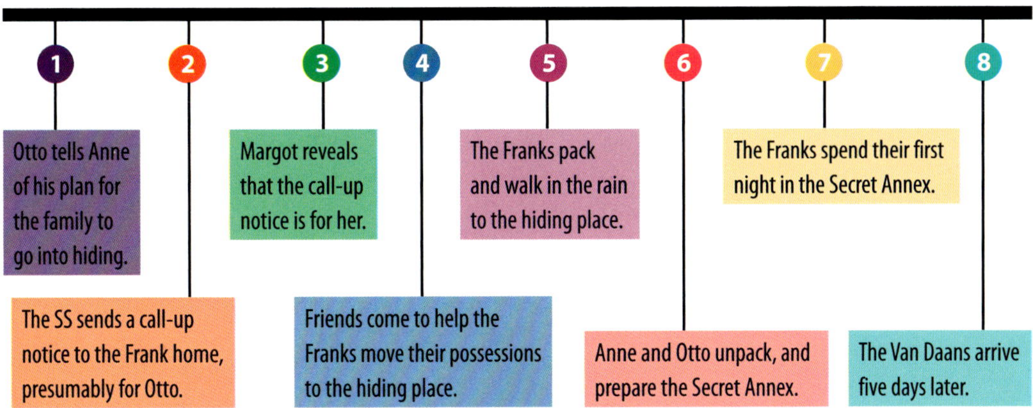

Literary Devices

Writers use a variety of literary devices to tell their stories. Most of these devices are either literary elements or literary techniques. The specific literary techniques a writer uses typically depend on the writer's unique style.

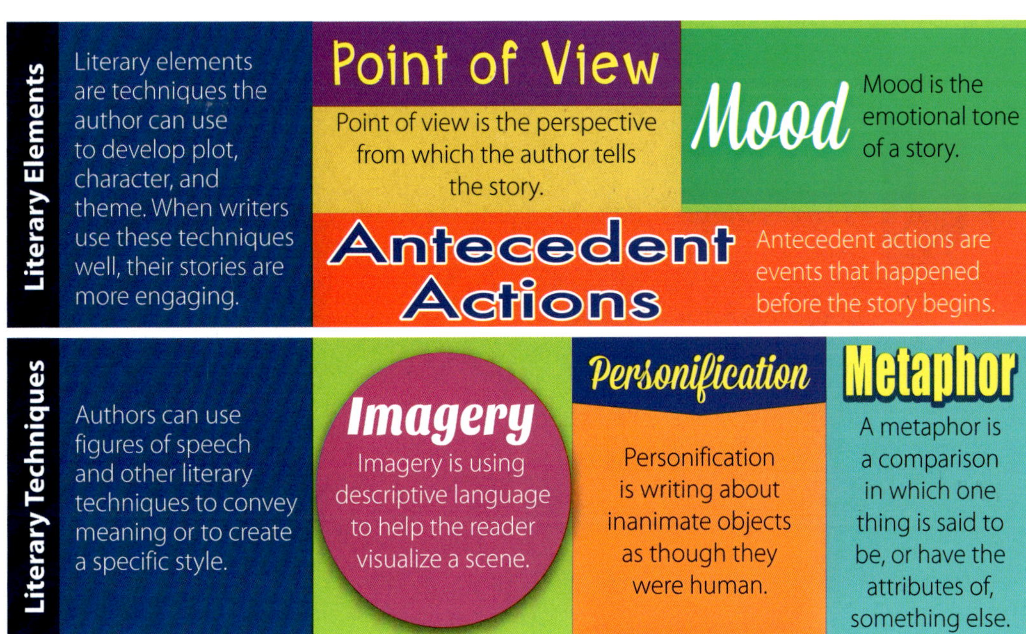

ACTIVITIES

Video

Reclaiming Anne Frank's Diary as Literature

Discover more about Anne's diary by watching this interview with author Francine Prose.

1. In the video, Prose notes that Anne thought of herself as a writer, and considered her writing to be a work of literature. How does this fact affect your understanding of the diary? Why is it important to consider Anne's writing as literature? What evidence from the diary supports the argument that Anne intended for it to be published and read?
2. Prose believes that the diary was consciously crafted, due to Anne's use of techniques such as dialogue, narration, passages of reflection, and dramatized scenes. What impact do these techniques have on the reader? Identify an example of each technique, citing specific passages from the diary.

More

Examples of Literary Techniques from the Diary

Analyze the author's use of literary techniques and how they contribute to the narrative of the diary.

1. Choose one literary technique used in the diary. In what particular way did the author use this literary technique? How effective was its usage?
2. What arguments can be made for the use of your chosen literary technique in a text? If this technique were overused or underutilized, what effect might it have on an author's work?

Theme in the Diary

Theme is the message or meaning in a work of literature. It is not the same as a moral, which tells the reader how to think or behave. Rather, it is a general observation about human nature. In some stories, the theme is stated directly. In others, the theme is subtly hinted at, leaving the reader to interpret the story's message.

Authors use various strategies to express theme. The repetition of thematic words and phrases is one technique. Having the narrator or other characters pose rhetorical questions is another. In *The Diary of a Young Girl*, Anne Frank asks rhetorical questions and makes direct thematic statements.

Theme and purpose

Anne was explicit about the purpose of her diary. She wanted it to be like having a friend and confidante. What stands out in Anne's diary is her optimism. Her writing was a way to keep her spirits up during the difficult and fearful years of her confinement. Anne later planned to publish her diary to inform others of her ordeal.

Major Themes of *The Diary of a Young Girl*

Even though Anne wrote her diary in the shadow of World War II and the Holocaust, her themes are inward-looking, and reflect the cares of a young girl between the ages of 13 and 15. Like many young people, she is preoccupied with the themes of growing up, happiness, and self-determination. As she struggles with typical adolescent concerns, Anne becomes a human face of the Holocaust and a symbol of all its innocent victims.

Growing Up

"I have now reached the stage that I can live entirely on my own, without Mummy's support or anyone else's for that matter. But it hasn't just happened in a night; it's been a bitter, hard struggle and I've shed many a tear, before I became as independent as I am now. You can laugh at me and not believe me, but that can't harm me. I know that I'm a separate individual and I don't feel in the least bit responsible to any of you. I am only telling you this because I thought that otherwise you might think that I was underhand, but I don't have to give an account of my deeds to anyone but myself."

Friday, 5 May, 1944, *The Diary of a Young Girl*

ACTIVITIES

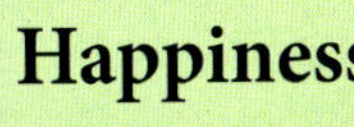

Happiness

"Riches can all be lost, but that happiness in your own heart can only be veiled, and it will still bring you happiness again, as long as you live. As long as you can look fearlessly up into the heavens, as long as you know that you are pure within, and that you will still find happiness."

Wednesday, 23 February, 1944, *The Diary of a Young Girl*

Anne Frank

Self-determination

"Quite honestly, I can't imagine how anyone can say: 'I'm weak,' and then remain so. After all, if you know it, why not fight against it, why not try to train your character? The answer was: 'Because it's so much easier not to!' This reply rather discouraged me. Easy? Does that mean that a lazy, deceitful life is an easy life? Oh no, that can't be true, it mustn't be true, people can so easily be tempted by slackness…and by money."

Thursday, 6 July, 1944, *The Diary of a Young Girl*

Secondary Themes

Secondary themes are those that are repeated less often and are not emphasized as strongly. These themes can add richness and complexity to a story, and give readers a deeper understanding of it. In *The Diary of a Young Girl*, some of the secondary themes that Anne Frank explores are prejudice, family, guilt, and the role of women in society.

Weblink

What Is Theme & Why Does It Matter?

Evaluate the article discussing what theme is and why it is important.

1. Do you think that the themes of *The Diary of Anne Frank* fit the article writer's definition of theme? If so, provide specific examples to support your position. If not, how would you modify this definition to better fit the themes of the text?
2. How do the themes Anne uses help readers to connect with her story? What does the diary help readers to understand about the human condition?

More

Major and Secondary Themes

Analyze the author's development of themes over the course of the diary.

1. Choose a secondary theme from this spread and analyze its appearances in the diary. How does this theme first emerge? Which is the most poignant example of this theme in the diary?
2. What particular commentary might the author be making about life as a result of this theme's presence in the text? Explain and defend your ideas.
3. Choose a major theme presented on pages 16–17. In what ways does your chosen secondary theme relate to this major theme? Does it deepen or detract from the major theme? How or in what way?

RUBRIC

Creating a Symbolism Poster

Students will choose one of the other symbols listed on page 19 and analyze its role in the diary. They will then create a poster to present their analysis. An exemplary symbolism poster will meet the following criteria.

- Presents a clear purpose that is conveyed throughout the poster
- Shows an understanding of the concept of symbolism and the role it has in the diary
- Provides an in-depth analysis of what the symbol represents
- Discusses the role the symbol has in the diary
- Clearly indicates where the symbol appears in the diary
- Uses specific, detailed examples from the text to support the analysis
- Makes clear connections to the text
- Properly integrates all quotations
- Organizes the information in a logical, easy-to-read manner
- Includes high-quality graphics that relate to the symbol and effectively enhance understanding of the topic
- Features clear and concise writing
- Uses correct spelling, grammar, and punctuation
- Clearly labels items of importance
- Headings and subheadings are clear and easy to read
- Uses layout to creatively enhances the information
- Creates a poster that is attractive in terms of layout, design, and organization
- Shows a strong effort by the student

Symbolism in the Diary

A symbol is something that has meaning beyond its literal definition. This can be a word, an image, an object, or an action. Writers use symbols to develop their themes, and to add layers of meaning to their work.

Some symbols are widely understood. Hearts and roses, for example, symbolize love in North American popular culture, while skulls symbolize death. Other symbols are specific to the work in which they appear. The sound of the beating heart in Edgar Allen Poe's story *The Tell-Tale Heart*, for example, does not symbolize love, but rather the narrator's guilty conscience. To interpret symbols in literature, readers sometimes need to make inferences based on their understanding of an author's work, and of broader literary and cultural traditions.

Writing and Freedom

"I want to get on; I can't imagine that I would have to lead the same sort of life as Mummy and Mrs. Van Daan and all the women who do their work and are then forgotten. I must have something besides a husband and children, something that I can devote myself to! I want to go on living even after my death! And therefore I am grateful to God for giving me this gift, this possibility of developing myself and of writing, of expressing all that is in me."

Tuesday, 4 April, 1944, *The Diary of a Young Girl*

The Diary as a Symbol

Anne's diary and the act of writing have symbolic meaning. The diary itself symbolizes friendship and the normal life Anne left behind when she went into hiding. Anne's letters to "Kitty" remind the reader of the peers and confidantes who are absent in her life. Writing symbolizes freedom for Anne—both a means of mental escape from the Secret Annex, and freedom from the limited roles to which she sees her mother and Mrs. Van Daan confined.

Anne's Diary as a Symbol

Other Symbols in the Diary

Peter Wessel

Before Anne went into hiding, she had a crush on a boy named Peter Wessel. On January 6, 1944, she writes of a vivid dream she had about this boy—a dream that leaves a lasting impression. Even though Anne forms a romantic attachment with Peter Van Daan, his weak character disappoints her. Peter Wessel, on the other hand, comes to symbolize her ideal love.

The View from the Attic

Anne and the others in the Secret Annex spent two years without ever going outside. When Anne craved sunshine and nature, she made her way to the attic, which had the only window she could safely look out. The chestnut tree and the sliver of sky she saw from the attic window symbolized freedom and lifted her spirits.

Fountain Pen

Anne's fountain pen, with its chewed end, appears throughout the first half of the diary. Anne's grandmother sent her the gift when she was 9 years old, and it became a treasured possession. In the Secret Annex, the pen comes to symbolize not only Anne's beloved grandmother, but also the happy life Anne enjoyed before she went into hiding. The pen also symbolizes Anne's ambition to become a writer. When she accidentally puts the pen in the fire, it becomes a chilling reminder of the fate Anne and the others hope to escape—cremation in Nazi concentration camps.

ACTIVITIES

More

What Symbols Appear in the Diary?

Assess the author's use of symbolism in the diary.

1. Choose a sample passage from the chart and analyze what it represents. For which character is this symbol the most poignant in the diary? For which character is the symbol least poignant? Argue your opinions with clear reasons.
2. How is this symbol used or reflected in the diary's themes? Illustrate the ways in which the author's use of language deepens or weakens the meaning of the symbol. Explain and defend your ideas.

Weblink

The Complete Guide to Symbolism

Examine the blog post discussing the usage of symbolism in literature.

1. Contrast and compare examples of analytical descriptions of feelings and sensory descriptions using symbolism from the diary. Which kind is more effective in the diary? Provide reasons for your ideas.
2. Should analytical descriptions play a considerable role in the language of a diary? Why or why not?

The Use of Language

An author's style is the sum of the choices he or she makes when writing. These choices encompass, among other things, diction, sentence structure, the use of figurative or literal language, a formal or informal register, point of view, and content. Authors make these choices according to their purpose and their audience. An author's purpose might be to persuade, entertain, inform, explain, or describe. Readers vary in their individual identities, background knowledge, reading abilities, and values. Writers must keep all these factors in mind as they craft their work.

Anne's Aspirations

"Is there anything more beautiful in the world than to sit before an open widow and enjoy nature, to listen to the birds singing, feel the sun on your cheeks and have a darling boy in your arms? It is so soothing and peaceful to feel his arms around me, to know that he is close by and yet to remain silent, it can't be bad, for this tranquility is good. Oh, never to be disturbed again, not even by Mouschi."

Wednesday, 19 April, 1944,
The Diary of a Young Girl

Anne Frank

Purpose and Style in *The Diary of a Young Girl*

When Anne Frank began writing her diary, she imagined it as a friend with whom she could privately share her thoughts, feelings, and experiences. In 1944, she and the others in the Secret Annex heard a radio broadcast announcing the Dutch government's intention to gather diaries and other documents after the war, in order to preserve and share the experience of the Dutch people during this period. This announcement inspired Anne to rewrite her diary as a novel for publication.

Stylistic Choices in *The Diary of a Young Girl*

Point of View

Like most diaries, *The Diary of a Young Girl* is written mainly from the first person point of view. The reader sees events exclusively through Anne's eyes. By addressing her diary entries to Kitty, she introduces a second person point of view. Adding a "you" to her narrative creates a sense of intimacy for the reader. Reading the diary is like hearing a close friend confess her deepest secrets.

Idioms

An idiom is a phrase of figurative language that has become a common saying. Anne uses idiomatic expressions throughout her diary. Phrases such as "The children especially are so dirty you wouldn't want to touch them with a barge pole" add vividness to the writing and give the reader a sense of Anne's unique voice. The approachable, everyday language helps readers relate to Anne as an ordinary girl.

Rhetorical Questions

Rhetorical questions are those that are asked without expectation of an answer. Writers often ask such questions to provoke thought or to emphasize a point. Anne peppered her diary with rhetorical questions. In the earlier entries, they were conversational asides to Kitty. Later in the diary, Anne's rhetorical questions were more introspective, reflecting her maturity and increasing self-awareness.

Anne wrote her diary in **Dutch**, the language of the Netherlands.

Anne's original diary had a **red-and-green** checked cover.

When Anne rewrote her diary for publication, she used **215 sheets** of paper.

ACTIVITIES

Document

Life in the Secret Annex
Analyze this review by Meyer Levin published in *The New York Times* on October 6, 1996.

1. How does the fact that Anne's diary is written as events are happening affect the pace of the story? What might be different if it were written retrospectively instead? Explain your answer.
2. Levin calls Anne "a born writer." How does her use of language throughout the diary support this claim? Cite passages from the text.

Weblink

Rhetorical Question
Learn more about rhetorical questions and their use in literature by reading this article.

1. How do Anne's rhetorical questions reflect her maturity and increasing self-awareness? Give specific examples from the diary.
2. Are rhetorical questions in literature as important as they are in daily language? Why do you think so? Give evidence to support your opinion.

RUBRIC

Analyzing a Video

Students will watch and assess a video related to a component of the diary, and write an analysis of the video. An exemplary video analysis will meet the following criteria.

- Identifies the purpose of the video
- Identifies the intended audience of the video
- Describes how the content of the video is presented
- Summarizes the information and opinions presented in the video
- Analyzes the quality of the content presented in the video
- Assesses the effectiveness of the video
- Discusses the technical aspects of the video and whether or not these enhance the content
- Determines whether the images and graphics used in the video relate to the content
- Determines whether the video is easy to follow and understand
- Gives the analysis a clear and consistent purpose
- Organizes the analysis in a logical, effective manner
- Presents a strong, clear argument about the video
- Provides strong and accurate details to support the argument about the video
- Considers other perspectives on the purpose and effectiveness of the video
- Makes connections between the video and the diary
- Properly integrates quotations from the video
- Cites all sources used in the analysis

Impact of the Diary at the Time of Publishing

Liberated from Auschwitz in 1945, Otto Frank returned to Amsterdam. He had learned of his wife's death, but still hoped to find his daughters alive. After placing ads in newspapers and talking to survivors, he learned that Anne and Margot had died in Bergen-Belsen. Miep Gies and Bep Voskuijl, helpers of the Secret Annex group, had gathered Anne's notebooks and papers after the group was arrested. Upon learning that Otto was the only member of the Frank family to survive, Miep gave these documents to him.

Publishing the Diary

Otto typed Anne's handwritten entries himself. A historian read the manuscript and wrote an article about it for a Dutch newspaper. Publishers were interested, and the publishing house Contact took on the project. The first **edition** of Anne's diary, bearing the title *Het Achterhuis: Dagbrieven van 14 juni 1942 tot 1 augustus 1944* (The Secret Annex: Diary Letters from June 14, 1942 to August 1, 1944), was published on June 25, 1947.

The Diary's First Reader

Otto and Anne were close, but what his daughter revealed in her diary surprised him. Her thoughts and feelings were deeper than he had imagined. Otto had not known about Anne's love of nature or how seeing the chestnut tree through the attic window had delighted her. The diary revealed how harshly Anne had judged her mother and how she later regretted her unkind words. Otto also discovered how much Anne criticized herself and learned of her ambition to publish the diary. After some hesitation, he resolved to make her wish come true.

Sharing Anne's Work

Otto gave the first copies of the book to friends and family, the Dutch prime minister, and the Dutch royal family. The first edition sold out quickly in the Netherlands. The first translation into English appeared in 1952, when the diary was made available the United States and Great Britain. The book gained worldwide acclaim, and was translated into 34 languages between 1953 and 1969.

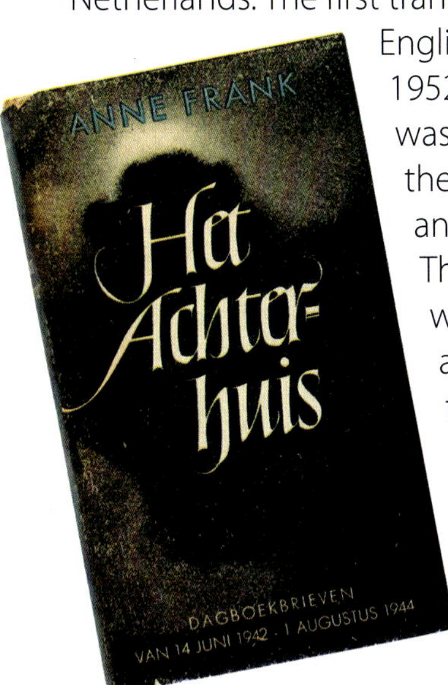

Reviews

In the Netherlands, The Secret Annex received enthusiastic reviews. Critics remarked on the moving story, and the clarity and authenticity of Anne's voice. In the United States, publishers were reluctant to take on the diary at first. When Doubleday released a modest 5,000 copies, a favorable review in The New York Times prompted the printing of an additional 60,000 copies.

Adapting the Diary

In the 1950s, *The Diary of a Young Girl* was adapted into both a play and a film. The play, written by American playwrights Frances Goodrich and Albert Hackett, opened in New York City on October 5, 1955. Critics lauded the work. It won a Tony Award, a Pulitzer Prize, and a New York Critics' Circle Award. In 1958, director George Stevens made the play into a movie, which won three Oscars. The Dutch royal family attended the film's Netherlands **premiere**.

ACTIVITIES

Video

Otto Frank talks about Anne's diary

Find out more about the discovery of Anne's diary by watching this video.

1. In the video, Otto Frank says that he was surprised by the deep thoughts Anne had when he read her diary. Why do you think Anne was only able to reveal her true self in her diary? How does reading about Anne and her experiences inspire confidence and hope, as Otto says?
2. Anne's father declares that in order "to build up a future, you have to know the past." What does this mean to you? Why is it so important to remember and talk about the events of the past? How does Anne's diary help contribute to this important discussion?

Document

Read TIME's Original Book Review for Anne Frank's Diary

Find out more about the diary's initial critical reception in this *Time* article by Lily Rothman, published on June 25, 2015.

1. The original 1952 review calls Anne's diary "one of the most moving stories that anyone, anywhere, has manged to tell about World War II." What is it about Anne's story that resonates with readers around the world? What effect would her story have if it were told from another point of view, such as her father's?
2. How have opinions of Anne's diary changed over the last seven decades? In what ways are they the same? Why do you think this is the case?

RUBRIC

Writing a Review

Students will write a review of the diary. An exemplary review will meet the following criteria.

- Grabs the reader's attention with a creative headline
- Begins with an engaging lead to pull the reader into the article
- Introduces the title of the diary, the author, and the genre
- Provides a brief plot description that does not give away the entire story, and makes the reader want to learn more about the diary
- Supports arguments about the diary with accurate and detailed information
- Organizes the review and its arguments in a concise, clear, and logical manner
- Fits the format and style of a review
- Follows the conventions of print or online journalism
- Demonstrates creativity in their approach
- Writes with a unique, engaging voice and perspective
- Provides fresh insight into the diary
- Provides an honest, authentic opinion on the diary
- Gives a clear recommendation on the diary, backed up by specific textual evidence
- Uses correct spelling, grammar, and punctuation

Impact of the Diary Now

The Diary of a Young Girl is one of the world's most popular and widely read books. One reason for its enduring appeal is Anne's optimism, which triumphs over her moments of fear and despair. The diary is relatable to many young readers as well. Anne wrote candidly about her entry into adolescence and family conflicts. People also still read the diary because Anne was a skilled writer. She knew how to use humor and suspense, and her writing was direct and full of energy and pathos.

Today, *The Diary of a Young Girl* has been **translated** into more than **70 languages**.

More than 25 million copies of *The Diary of a Young Girl* **have been sold to date**.

In the **United States**, 10 publishers **rejected** *The Diary of a Young Girl* before it made it to press.

Anne Frank House

In 1957, the global success of *The Diary of a Young Girl* prompted a group of Amsterdam citizens to create the Anne Frank Foundation. The foundation's goal was to save the building at 263 Prinsengracht from demolition. With support from the mayor of Amsterdam and the University of Amsterdam, the foundation renovated Anne Frank House and opened it to the public in 1960. Today, the house is a museum that features Anne's writings, artifacts from the people in hiding, permanent displays, and temporary exhibits. More than 1 million people from around the world visit Anne Frank House each year.

The Diary of Anne Frank as a Play

During its original two-year run on Broadway, from 1955 to 1957, the play was performed 717 times. It was performed another 221 times during a revival from November 1997 to June 1998. Actress Natalie Portman played the role of Anne. Proceeds from the revival supported the Survivors of the Shoah Visual History Foundation, founded by film director Steven Spielberg. Today, theater companies continue to include the play in their production calendars.

Anne Frank Schools

In 1957, the Montessori school Anne Frank attended in Amsterdam became the first school to be named in her honor. Schools that wish to adopt Anne Frank's name must register with the Anne Frank Foundation. Anne Frank schools honor the educational value of Anne's diary. The foundation expects these schools to teach the values of equality, justice, and mutual respect, to encourage students to read Anne's diary, and to discuss discrimination during World War II and in the present day. They must also spread Anne's thoughts and exchange ideas with other schools in the network. Today, there are more than 270 Anne Frank schools in 18 countries.

ACTIVITIES

Video

The Diary of Anne Frank
Watch this video interview about the 2018 production of *The Diary of Anne Frank* by the Harrell Performing Arts Theatre.

1. In the video, it is proposed that Anne Frank's story can help teach people about tolerance and compassion. How does the diary accomplish this? Is it true that Anne's story is "as relevant now as it was 70 years ago"? Why do you think this is the case?
2. Jillian Harper, who portrays Anne in the play, says she felt a connection with Anne when she first read her diary. Why is Anne's diary so relatable to young readers, even today? How does this fact exemplify Anne's skill as a writer? Support your answer with specific examples.

Document

Anne Frank: The Diary of a Young Girl by Anne Frank – review
Analyze the review from *The Guardian*, published on September 28, 2015.

1. What is the tone of the review? Who is the intended audience, and is this review appropriate for that audience? Explain why you think so by analyzing the topics covered in the review and the overall recommendation that is given at the end of it.
2. The reviewer claims that the story's most important message is that all people have the right to live in freedom. How does the diary convey this message? What other lessons do you take away from the diary?

RUBRIC

Creating a Timeline

Students will explore a topic related to the diary and create a timeline to present their research on historical events connected to this topic. An exemplary timeline will meet the following criteria.

- Includes the most significant events pertaining to the topic to be compared and analyzed
- Includes interesting events
- Uses accurate information for all events, including date, location, and major details
- Orders the events in a chronological sequence
- Describes each event with accurate, vivid, and specific details
- Presents the topic from three or more perspectives
- Inspires the reader to ask thoughtful questions regarding the events and perspectives presented in the timeline
- Uses correct spelling, grammar, and punctuation
- Presents the timeline in a visually attractive and striking manner
- Presents the timeline in a neat, organized manner that is logical and easy to follow
- Uses creativity to present the timeline in an engaging manner
- Effectively communicates the historical information relating to the topic
- Supports each event with reliable sources
- Expresses a clear purpose for creating the timeline
- Enhances the reader's understanding of the topic
- Includes a correctly formatted bibliography of all sources used to create the timeline

Perspectives on Genocide

The term **genocide** was coined in 1944 by Raphael Lemkin, a Polish lawyer. Lemkin was writing not only about the systemic murder of Jews during World War II, but also of killings of other targeted groups throughout history. In 1945, the United Nations (UN) was founded. The UN General Assembly officially recognized genocide as a crime in 1946, during its first session.

Timeline of Genocide Around the World

1200s

1900s

1209–1229 The Albigensian Crusade is the Roman Catholic Church's attempt to destroy members of the heretical Cathar sect in Languedoc, France. Roughly 1 million people die.

1904 In Namibia, German colonial rulers expel indigenous Herero and Nama people from their land, poison their wells, order troops to shoot them, and place survivors in concentration camps. Tens of thousands die.

1915–1922 The systemic massacre of Armenian people by the Ottoman Empire results in up to 1.5 million deaths.

1933–1945 The Nazis murder 6 million European Jews during the Holocaust. They also target Roma, homosexuals, disabled people, and religious dissidents, among others.

1948 The United Nations Convention on the Prevention and Punishment of the Crime of Genocide defines the crime of genocide. Today, the convention has been ratified by 149 countries.

ACTIVITIES

The crime of genocide has two components, which are intention and action. If a crime is to be classed as genocide, the perpetrators must deliberately target an ethnic, racial, national, or religious group with the intent to destroy that group. Genocidal actions include killing members of the targeted group, causing them grave physical or mental harm, preventing births within the group, taking the group's children from them, and imposing deadly living conditions on the group.

1992–1995 After Bosnia-Herzegovina declares independence from the former Yugoslavia, Bosnian Serb forces target Bosnian Muslim and Croatian civilians. Approximately 100,000 people—most of them Bosnian Muslims—are killed.

2003 The Sudanese government arms Arab militias to attack and kill members of the Fur, Masalit, and Zaghawa ethnic groups in the Darfur region of Sudan. Hundreds of thousands are killed, and more than 1 million are driven off their land.

2005 UN member nations accept the responsibility of protecting their own people from genocide and other mass crimes.

2000s

1994 Hutu nationalists in Rwanda incite the murder of up to 800,000 members of the Tutsi minority.

2014–Present The Islamic State kills, tortures, and enslaves thousands of Yazidi people—members of a religious minority—in Iraq.

Transparency–Timeline

Timeline of Genocide Around the World

Examine the historical and cultural contexts shown on the timeline. Then, contrast and correlate its elements with the themes and events presented in *The Diary of a Young Girl.*

1. In what ways can historical events, culture, and social mores influence a population's perspective on crimes such as genocide? How might these elements have shaped the way a reader in the late 1940s interpreted the diary?
2. How might the era in which Anne Frank wrote her diary have influenced its themes and settings? Where in the diary is this most evident? Explain your reasoning.
3. Which current events, changes in laws, new ideas, or political discussions are shaping people's reactions to mass crimes in the United States today? Which ideas and attitudes are still prevailing? Why?
4. How might current events and present perspectives affect the way a reader interprets the diary? Why is it important for readers to understand the era and context in which a text is written?

RUBRIC

Writing a Comparative Essay

Students will compare two literary devices used in the diary, and then write a comparative essay based on their analysis. An exemplary comparative essay will meet the following criteria.

- Consists of a one-paragraph introduction, three body paragraphs, and a one-paragraph conclusion
- Introduction includes an engaging lead statement about the topic of the essay, more detailed information about the diary, and a one-sentence thesis that specifically states the essay's argument
- Body paragraphs include a topic sentence that refers to the thesis and how the idea appears in the diary, a supporting sentence that points to this part of the diary, textual evidence of this idea from the diary, and analysis of this evidence
- Body paragraphs end with a transition to the next paragraph
- Conclusion refers to the topic of the essay and the three points presented in the body paragraphs, and restates the thesis
- Provides a thorough analysis of the literary devices in question
- Cites strong and thorough textual evidence to support analysis of what the diary says explicitly
- Presents a clear, specific thesis that indicates a high level of critical engagement
- Organizes ideas in a logical manner
- Communicates arguments in a clear, effective manner
- Properly integrates all quotations
- Correctly cites all sources used
- Correctly formats bibliography

Writing a Comparative Essay

Anne Frank engages readers with vivid character sketches, suspenseful moments, and thought-provoking themes in *The Diary of a Young Girl*. After studying the diary, write a comparative essay to explore how two literary devices are used in it. This could be a comparison of characters, themes, symbols, or settings. To write a comparative essay, you will need to formulate an argument. Your argument should clearly state how your compared elements are similar or different. Support your argument with valid reasoning and sufficient evidence from the diary.

How to Analyze and Compare Characters

Use the chart to guide your comparison of two characters in *The Diary of a Young Girl.*

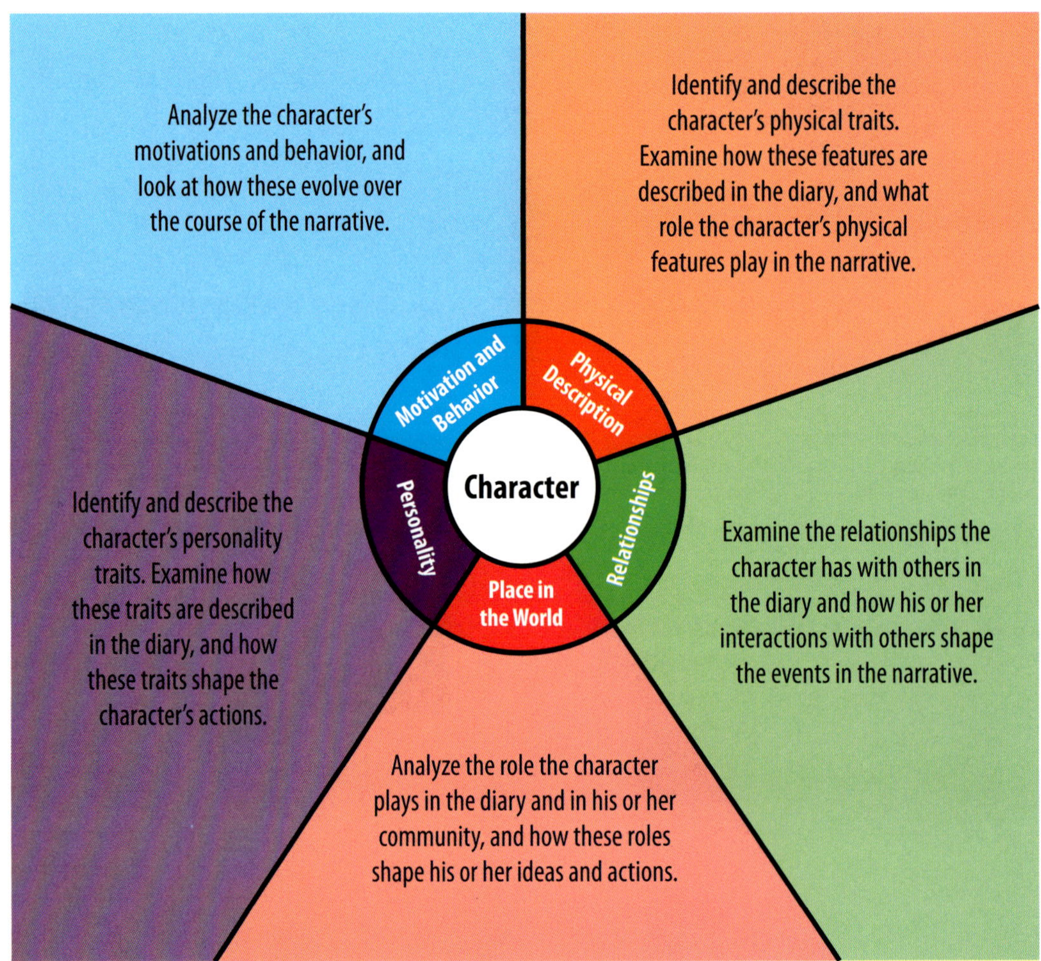

Comparing Mrs. Frank with Mrs. Van Daan

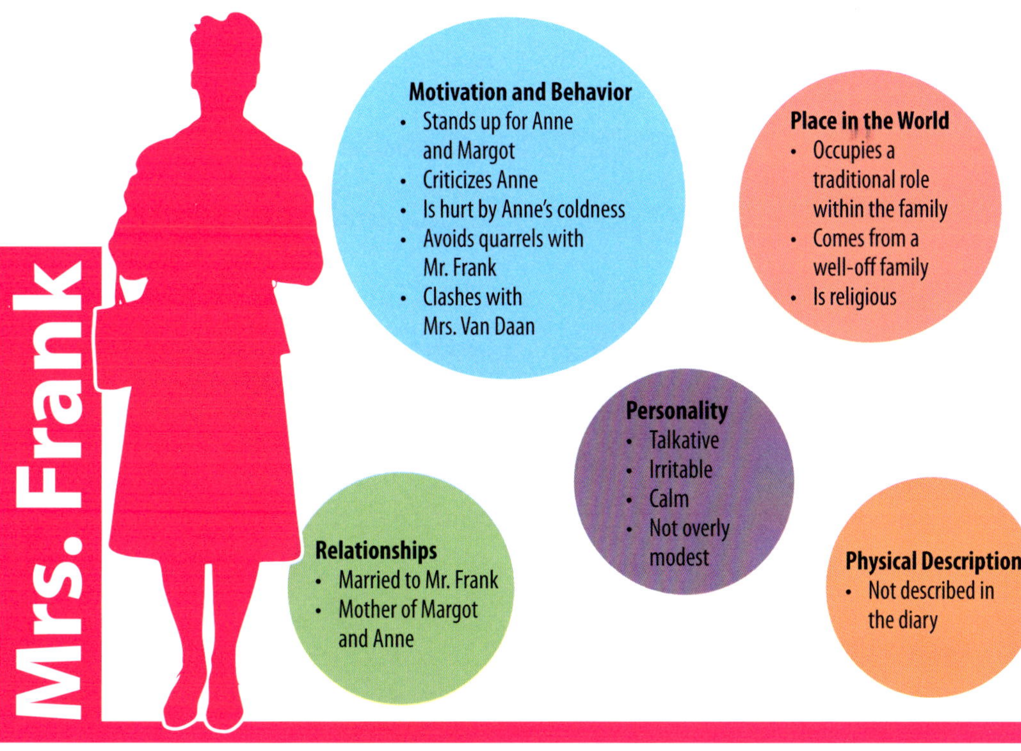

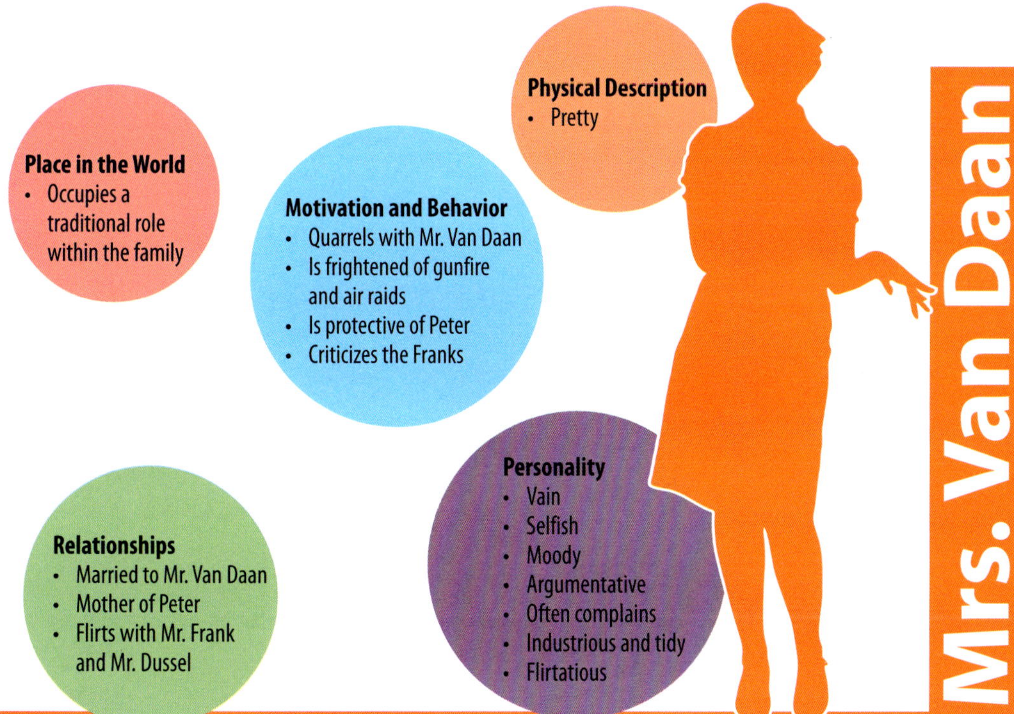

 More

Questions for Character Analysis

Analyze how specific character features, such as conflicts, motivations, relationships, place in the world, and personality affect the plot of *The Diary of a Young Girl*. Cite strong and thorough textual evidence to support your analysis of what the diary says explicitly as well as the inferences you may have drawn from the diary's setting, themes, and symbols.

Quiz Answers

1. A
2. C
3. A
4. C
5. D
6. B
7. B
8. A
9. C
10. C

Key Words

anti-Semitic: hostile to, or prejudiced against, people of Jewish ethnicity or religious beliefs

civilians: people who do not serve in the armed forces or on a police force

concentration camp: a place where large numbers of people are imprisoned, often to provide labor or await execution

dissidents: people who are opposed to the policies of an authoritarian state

edition: the number of copies of a publication made available at one time

genocide: the systemic killing of a people with the intent to wipe out a religious, ethnic, national, or racial group

Holocaust: the period of state-sponsored persecution of millions of Jews by Adolf Hitler and the Nazi regime, with the goal of exterminating Europe's Jewish population

intelligence: information of political or military value

minorities: groups of people who make up less than half of a population and are distinguished by race, ethnicity, religion, political beliefs, or other characteristics

Montessori school: a school following the teachings of Italian doctor Maria Montessori, typically focusing on emotional, physical, social, and cognitive development through interaction instead of direct instruction

persecution: severe punishment and cruel treatment, generally based on differences in ethnicity, religion, or political ideology

premiere: the first public viewing of a play, film, or other performance

racism: discrimination against people of a different race, or the belief that other races are inferior to one's own

refugees: people forced to leave their own country to escape war or persecution

regime: an authoritarian government

Literary Terms

action: everything that occurs in a narrative

antagonist: the character who stands in opposition to the protagonist

antecedent action: background events that take place before the first event in the plotline of a narrative

conflict: a struggle between two or more opposing forces, creating a tension that must be resolved

diarists: people who write diaries

diary: a written record of one's daily experiences and observations

dynamic characters: characters who change significantly over the course of a story

flashback: the narration of events that happened before the present moment in a story

narrative: a logically arranged series of events presented for an audience; a story

pathos: something in a work of art or literature that makes the audience feel intense emotion, such as pity or sadness

plot: the specific action that propels a story forward

point of view: the perspective from which a story is narrated

protagonist: the central character in a piece of fiction who must deal with a conflict and often undergoes some type of change as a result

rhetorical questions: statements posed as questions for emphasis, with no answer expected

settings: places and times in which the events of a story occur

static characters: characters who do not change significantly over the course of a story

style: the way an author uses words

symbolism: a stylistic device using symbols to represent and intensify concepts and ideas

theme: the underlying topic, idea, or position in a work that is often a general, universal statement about life

Index

A Raisin in the Sun 10
Aachen, Germany 4
Allied Forces 6, 8, 9
Amsterdam, Netherlands 4, 5, 6, 7, 22, 24, 25
Anne Frank Foundation 24, 25
Anne Frank schools 25
Auschwitz concentration camp 5, 22
Axis 9

Bergen-Belsen concentration camp 5, 22

Darfur, Sudan 27
Diary of Anne Frank, The 25
Dussel, Mr. 7, 11, 29

Europe 8, 9, 26

France 9, 23, 26
Frank, Anne 4, 5, 7, 8, 11, 12, 13, 14, 15, 16, 17, 18, 19, 20, 21, 22, 23, 24, 25, 28, 29
Frank, Edith 4, 5, 7, 13, 16, 18, 22, 29
Frank, Margot 4, 5, 7, 12, 15, 22, 29
Frank, Otto 4, 5, 7, 11, 12, 13, 15, 22, 23
Frankfurt am Main, Germany 4

genocide 26, 27
Germany 4, 5, 6, 7, 9
Gies, Miep 22
Goodrich, Frances 23
Great Britain 9, 23
Great Depression 9

Hackett, Albert 23
Harry Potter series 10
Hitler, Adolf 4, 9
Holocaust 9, 13, 16, 26

Into Thin Air 10
Iraq 27
Islamic State 27
Italy 9

Japan 9
Jews 4, 6, 7, 8, 9, 11, 26

Lemkin, Raphael 26

Macbeth 10

Nazis 6, 8, 9, 12, 19, 26
Netherlands 4, 5, 6, 8, 21, 23
North Sea 6

Ottoman Empire 26

Poland 5, 9
Portman, Natalie 25

Roma 9, 26
Rwanda 27

Secret Annex 5, 7, 8, 11, 13, 15, 18, 19, 20, 22
Slavs 9
Soviet Union 9
Stevens, George 23

Treaty of Versailles 9

United Nations 26
United States 9, 23, 24

Van Daan, Mr. 5, 7, 13, 15, 29
Van Daan, Mrs. 5, 7, 13, 15, 18, 29
Van Daan, Peter 5, 7, 13, 15, 19, 29

Wessel, Peter 19
Westerbork 5
World War I 9
World War II 6, 8, 9, 16, 25, 26

LIGHTBOX

SUPPLEMENTARY RESOURCES

Click on the plus icon ⊕ found in the bottom left corner of each spread to open additional teacher resources.

- Download and print the book's quizzes and activities
- Access curriculum correlations
- Explore additional web applications that enhance the Lightbox experience

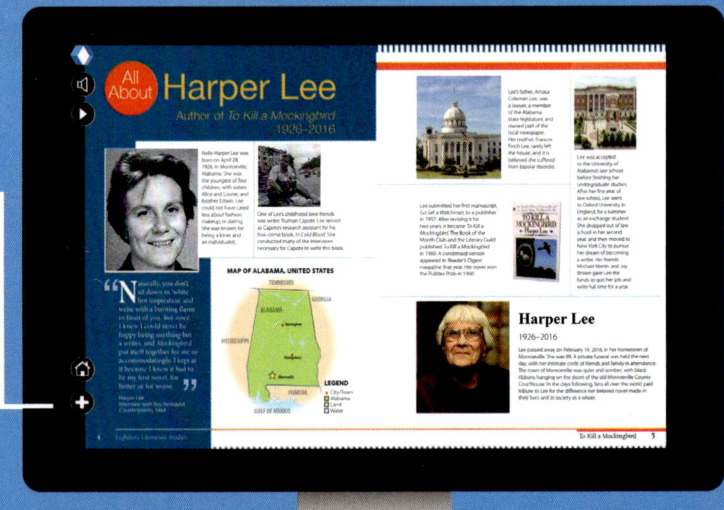

LIGHTBOX DIGITAL TITLES
Packed full of integrated media

VIDEOS

INTERACTIVE MAPS

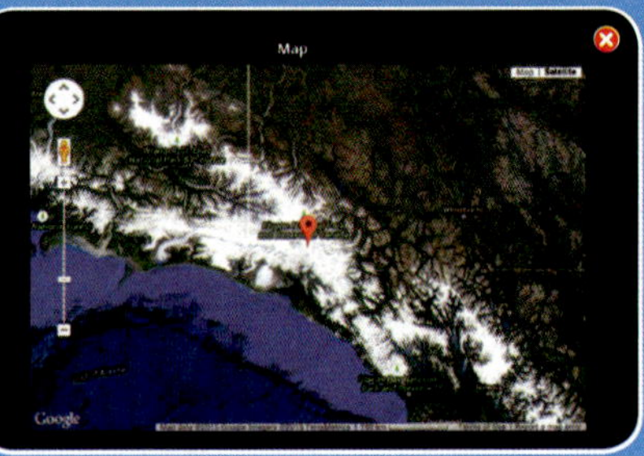

WEBLINKS

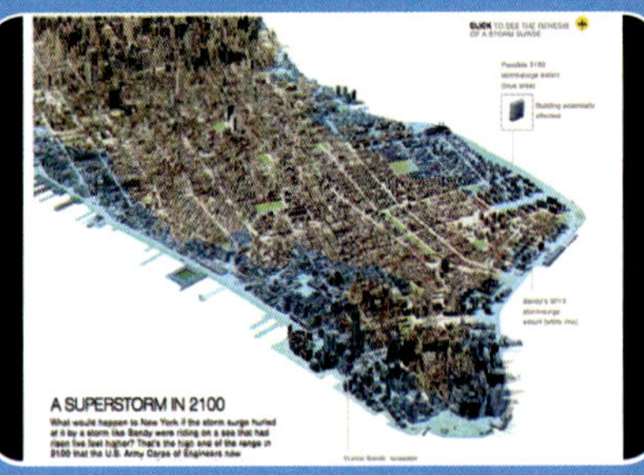

SLIDESHOWS

QUIZZES

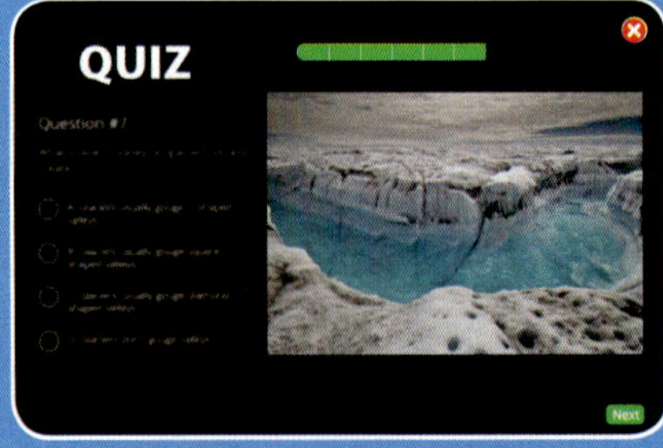

OPTIMIZED FOR

- ✓ TABLETS
- ✓ WHITEBOARDS
- ✓ COMPUTERS
- ✓ AND MUCH MORE!

Published by Smartbook Media Inc.
350 5th Avenue, 59th Floor New York, NY 10118
Website: www.openlightbox.com

Library of Congress Cataloging-in-Publication Data
Names: Lomberg, Michelle, author. | Gillespie, Katie, author.
Title: The diary of a young girl / Michelle Lomberg and Katie GIllespie.
Description: New York, NY : Smartbook Media Inc., 2018. | Series: Lightbox literature studies | Includes index.
Identifiers: LCCN 2017056749 (print) | LCCN 2017057246 (ebook) | ISBN 9781510537071 (Multi-User eBook) | ISBN 9781510537064 (hard cover : alk.paper)
Subjects: LCSH: Frank, Anne, 1929-1945. Achterhuis--Juvenile literature. | Frank, Anne, 1929-1945. Achterhuis--Study and teaching--Activity programs.
| Holocaust, Jewish (1939-1945)--Netherlands--Amsterdam--Juvenile literature. | Jews--Persecutions--Netherlands--Amsterdam--Juvenile literature. | Amsterdam (Netherlands)--Ethnic relations--Juvenile literature.
Classification: LCC DS135.N6 (ebook) | LCC DS135.N6 F7333885 2018 (print) | DDC 940.53/18092 [B] --dc23
LC record available at https://lccn.loc.gov/2017056749

Printed in Brainerd, Minnesota, United States
1 2 3 4 5 6 7 8 9 0 22 21 20 19 18

062018
121017

Editor: Katie Gillespie
Art Director: Terry Paulhus

The publisher acknowledges Getty Images, iStock, Alamy, and Wikimedia Commons as its primary image suppliers for this title.